AF364642

Becoming Her
Poems of Legacy and Love

Mridula Bhardwaj

Paperback ISBN: 978-93-5911-380-7
eBook ISBN: 978-93-5911-766-9

First Published in November, 2024

Published by Walnut Publication

(an imprint of Vyusta Ventures LLP)

www.walnutpublication.com

India

Unit# 909, 9th Floor, Wave Silver Tower, Sector-18, Noida - 201301

USA

1820 Avenue M #849, Brooklyn, NY 11230, United States of America

Distributed by

To My Dearest Mother

This book is my way of keeping you with me— not just in my memories, but for the world to see the beauty of who you are. Every word honors your love, strength, and wisdom, reflecting not only my heart, but those of your children, friends, and family.

To my siblings, your son-in-law, and daughters-in-law, who cherish you deeply, and encouraged me unconditionally. But special thanks to Digisha for letting me pen down my heart.

To your dear friends, siblings and family, whose admiration for you fills these pages and whose memories remind us of kindness.

Mom, you are not just a mother but a guiding force in the lives of all who know you. you've shaped us all, you live in our hearts and through these poems you will forever be in the world.

With all my love,
Your youngest, who will always be your shadow.

Preface

This memoir is a heartfelt tribute to my mother, whose love, strength, and wisdom have shaped the lives of all who know her. While it comes from my heart as her daughter, it reflects the voices of my siblings, her children-in-law, friends, and family - each touched by her presence.

Through these poems, I share the lessons, laughter, and love we've experienced with her. I tried to reflect my journey of seeing my mother as my world, then as the strictest figure, and now as my universe. Uncannily, I see her in both myself and my daughter, realizing I'm slowly becoming Her. My goal is to celebrate her not only in my memories but for the world to see the incredible woman she is. This book is a living testament to her legacy, one that will remain forever in our hearts.

To My Mother, From the Past till the Future

I stand on the edge of becoming a mother,
Heart swollen with dreams and fears to uncover,
But my thoughts, they wander—back to the past,
To a time when I was reckless and fast.

A teenager—so sure, so wild,
A whirlwind of moods, a defiant child.
I see your face, worn but so strong,
Holding me close when I was wrong.

How you weathered my storms with patience untold,
When I fought for my freedom, so selfish, so bold.
I see you, standing in the kitchen light,
Tired eyes soft, but your spirit bright.

The tears, the tantrums, the shouting and slamming,
The hours you spent just calmly examining,
Why I, with my heart set on things so unwise,
Refused to hear, refused your eyes.

I know now what I didn't see then—
The sacrifice, the worry, the places you've been.
How you held me close when I pushed you away,
How you never gave up, never asked me to stay.

And now, as I cradle this life in my hand,
I wonder, will I ever understand—
How you loved me so fiercely through all of my mess,
And how you made sure I felt truly blessed.

I can't help but feel the weight in my chest,
For the times I caused you such endless unrest.
For the moments when I was cruel and demanding,
And you, with grace, kept standing—standing.

Now, I see your love, the quiet kind,
The one that doesn't always speak but finds
A way to endure, to rise above,
A love that asks for nothing, just gives and gives.

So, as I become a mother, I know I will try,
To give as you gave, with a heart full of why.
For in your hands, I see what's true—
A mother's love is endless, and I owe it to you.

Poonam Rani - The Moonlit Heart

Poonam Rani, her name a light,
Like the full moon on a quiet night.
A name that shines, soft and bright,
She is the glow, the calm, the might.

Her eyes, so dark, so full, so deep,
With lashes long, like secrets keep.
In her gaze, the world feels still,
A silent love, a gentle will.

Her hair, like night, long and black,
Tied in a braid, no strand out of track.
Her smile, a beam, so pure, so wide,
With teeth so white, they cannot hide.

Dusky skin, with warmth and grace,
A quiet beauty lights her face.
A moonlit glow, serene and rare,
She walks with love, she walks with care.

To her father, she was "Poonu beta,"
His pride, his joy, his heart's umbrella.
To her mother, the sweetest one,
Her love as constant as the sun.

The third among five, yet always first,
In love, in duty, in giving thirst.
With Suresh, Naresh, Kusum and Sanjay, she shared her
heart,
A bond so strong, it would never part.

She worked the fields, helped with the cows,
In kitchen and home, she kept her vows.
A sister, a mother, a daughter, a friend,
Her love for her family has no end.

When she married, her world grew wide,
With my father, by her side.
Discipline strict, yet love was strong,
She learned to balance, the right the wrong.

Each meal she made, fresh and warm,
Each chore she did, with no alarm.
Two more children, five in total, she took in stride,
A mother of many, with love as her guide.

Late at night, she'd sew and bake,
Pickles and snacks, for others' sake.
She'd watch a film, just for a while,
A moment of peace, a quiet smile.

As an aanganwadi nurse, she cared
For every soul, for those who dared.
She learned from others, helped with grace,
Her kindness spread in every place.

She gave her heart, her food, her hand,
To those in need, to all the land.
Her love was simple, pure, and true,
A quiet soul, with much to do.

They say she's too good to be real,
Such kindness, how can one feel?
I laugh and smile, for I can see,
She's the moon, and that's just she.

In Haryana's heart, she lights the way,
Shaping futures, day by day.
Through government's touch, schools thrive and grow,
A brighter tomorrow, she helps to sow.

Poonam Rani, the light,
Her love a flame that burns so bright.
She's not just a mother, but a moon,
A quiet glow that does not end too soon.

The Innocence of Her Beginnings

I hear the stories told with smiles and sighs,
Of the girl who grew up with soft, wide eyes—
The mother I know, but not quite the same,
Before the weight of the world had called her name.

They say she was fragile, a bird with no wings,
With a heart that would bloom like the softest of springs.
Her parents speak gently of days long ago,
Of a child who gave warmth wherever she'd go.

She'd gather the children, the lost and the stray,
And feed them with kindness, without a delay.
Her hands, so small, could weave magic from thread,
Knitting, and stitching, and making things spread.
She'd learn from the masters, by watching their hands,
An artist of patience, in life's simple strands.

Her siblings all speak of the care she would give,
How she'd tend to them gently, how they'd always forgive
Her quiet resolve, the way she would be,
The protector, the listener, so tender, so free.
Her cousins, her neighbors, would all come to find
That her love was as vast as the sky—so kind.

Then one friend, a girl with eyes full of glee,
Remembers the day they were children, carefree.
Outside the school gate, a fruit vendor stood,
Selling berries that everyone thought were so good.
They'd pooled together a few coins to buy,
But the seller was busy—no fruit, no reply.

They asked a boy standing near by the stall,
To run with their money and buy them it all.; In
But the boy took the coins and dashed down the lane,
Leaving the girls standing, in growing disdain.

Her friend, outraged, yelled and sobbed with great grief,
But my mother—oh, she could not bring relief.
She stood there, silent, in a cloud of pure shock,
Her eyes filled with tears that refused to unlock.
And when the boy returned, to give back the coin,
Her friend rushed back to class, anger her only line.

But my mother? She wept, not for herself,
But for the broken trust—innocence on a shelf.
Such a fragile soul, not yet knowing the fight,
And how could she? She still saw the world in pure light.

Then there was the time when her brother, so dear,
Shouted in anger, his voice full of fear.
She, the helper, the one who would care,
Tried so hard to be there, but then—despair.
He yelled at her sharply, for something, I know not,
But her heart, so tender, couldn't bear the thought.

That night she burned with a fever, so high,
Her body too weak, her spirit awry.
How did such a gentle soul bear this weight,
When all she had done was love and create?

Now, here I stand, wondering still,
How did this kind, fragile girl learn to fill
The shoes of the woman I see every day—
The fearless, the strong, who won't turn away?

When did her heart shift from innocence pure,
To a strength that could stand, that could love and endure?
How did she grow from the girl who once wept,
To the mother who stands, no longer swept—
But steady and strong, and so full of grace,
A woman whose courage no storm can erase?

I look at her now, and I still can't believe,
That the fragile girl with tears on her sleeve,
Became the woman who taught me to stand,
With a heart full of courage and an open hand.

And as I step forward, with a child of my own,
I carry with me the seeds she has sown—
The innocence she once was, the strength she's become,
The wisdom she holds, in her silence, is one.

The Grandmother's Love

Now I see her—in a different kind of light,
Not the woman who once stood in quiet fight,
But a grandmother, joyful and full of grace,
With laughter and warmth etched upon her face.

She sits in the middle of her four little loves,
Prabhav, Trisha, Misha and Digisha
The grandkids who circle her like stars above.
Three girls, so lively, one boy full of cheer,
All dear to her heart, with hearts so sincere.

I've never seen her quite like this before,
A child once more, playing and exploring the floor.
She tells stories, each one so grand,
Tales of animals, of magic, and distant lands.

She sings songs about morals, about right and wrong,
Filling their minds with wisdom through playful song.
Animal rhymes, fairies, and dreams in the sky,
She dances with joy as the hours slip by.
She teaches them lessons in the most subtle way,

With patience that blooms like the flowers of May.
When they're unwell, she becomes their own cure,
Tender and soft, her love ever pure.

In wellness, she's there with the brightest of smiles,
And her care goes on for miles and miles.
She knits them sweaters, so cozy and bright,
Warming their hearts, with threads woven tight.

She's learned new styles, new dresses to make,
Creating with love each stitch, each break.
For each granddaughter, she dreams up a plan—
Before every festival, a gift from her hand.

She listens to them all with such patient grace,
No story too small, no word misplaced.
And when they speak of their hopes and their fears,
She holds them close and wipes away tears.

She challenges herself, with courage anew,
Taking on lessons, both old and new.
A language once foreign, now she grasps it with pride,
Teaching the kids with joy by her side.

Her love doesn't stop at their day-to-day needs,
She's laid down the groundwork for their future deeds.
Her plans stretch beyond the horizon so wide,
Her vision a beacon that will always guide.

She's cheerful and fun, but responsible still,
A balance of joy and unbreakable will.
She takes life as it comes, with grace in her stride,
A lesson to me on how to live with pride.

As a teacher, I watch her, and I learn,
How to listen, how to love, how to wait for my turn.
Her actions speak louder than any words could say,
She teaches with love in the gentlest way.

She's the mother I know, but more than I see,
A grandmother whose love grows endlessly.
Her heart is a well that never runs dry,
A guide to her grandchildren as years pass by.

And as I watch her, I can't help but smile,
For the woman I see has traveled a mile.
From innocence lost to strength and grace,
Now she's a grandmother, lighting the place.

There's so much to learn, just by being near,
Her love is a lesson, so pure and so clear.
In her I see a mother, a teacher, a friend,
A love that will last, that will never end.

The Fire of Change

She'd lived in a house with walls so tight,
Where chores and care were her guiding light.
Cooking and cleaning, cattle and kin,
Her days were marked by the hum of life's spin.

Then came the day, a flame burned bright,
Her husband gone, swallowed by night.
The world was cold, too harsh to bear,
She crumbled, lost in grief and despair.

But through the smoke, her children's cries,
Manish, like stone, with tearless eyes.
Sidharth wept, his heart in pain,
And little Mridula waited in vain.

The door stood open, no scooter came,
And in that silence, she felt the flame.
The fire of grief, of loss so deep,
Was burning her soul, denying her sleep.

But as she looked at their innocent faces,
A quiet strength began to trace its places.
She breathed for the first time, deep and slow,
And thought of the future, what she'd sow.

I must live, for them, I must stay,
She whispered to herself, and found her way.
A dream of education, for her children bright,
But how? How to bring them into the light?

With family by her side, Kusum's hand to hold,
She gathered courage, quiet yet bold.
To Panchkula, with hope and fear,
A city unknown, yet drawing near.

Three kids in tow, a job to find,
A clerk's position, with nerves combined.
Twenty-five kilometers, curvy roads ahead,
A river to cross, by foot she tread.

No bus to ride, no shortcut clear,
But with suman by her side, she marched with faith,
sincere.
To the school, where learning awaited,
A journey uncertain, yet unabated.

Her first day came, no skills to show,
But honesty, her heart would grow.
"I know nothing," she said with grace,
"But I will learn, at my own pace."

The principal, Mrs. Gupta, smiled and said,
"That's the heart of a worker, not misled.
A hunger to learn, to grow, to rise,
A humble spirit, a truth that never dies."

Those words, a seed planted deep,
Gave her the strength to no longer weep.
The road was hard, the work was tough,
But for her children, she'd never had enough.

Panchkula became a city of dreams,
Not just of struggles, but of quiet beams.
A mother's love, a will unbroken,
Her journey had only just begun, unspoken.

राजकीय उच्च विद्यालय धतागड़ा

The Legacy

I watched my daughter, bright and fair,
Charming the world with love to share.
Her laughter echoed, her eyes so wise,
And in that moment, I realized—
How much of her, I see in me,
How much of me, I learned to be,
From the one who shaped me with gentle hands,
My mother, who built my life's foundations.

When strangers praised her joy and grace,
I turned to my husband, and saw his face—
A proud smile, full of love and pride,
And in my heart, I felt a tide
Of gratitude, of thanks untold,
For the woman whose hands, strong yet bold,
Had woven me from threads of care,
Her love and wisdom everywhere.

I thought of days long passed, and true,
Of how my mother taught me too:
To share with those who had no voice,
To give what I could, not by choice,
But by the grace of simple acts,
Of kindness, giving, and selfless facts.
She fed the hungry, the stray, the lost—
Her heart, so open, no matter the cost.

She taught us to forgive, to bend,
Like branches with the weight of friends—
To take the stones that others throw,
And still let kindness gently flow.
Her strength was found in letting go,
In standing tall, but not alone.

She wasn't much of the learned, but so wise, you see,
With questions wide as the open sea.
She'd ask us what the stars were for,
What made the sun rise up once more.
And though her book was small and torn,
Her mind was sharp, her spirit born
To teach, to question, to seek, to grow,
And that's how I learned what I know.

She showed us how to stand, and rise,
With hands that worked, and humble eyes.
We washed the dishes, swept the floor,
And learned that effort is worth much more
Than any gift that comes too fast—
It's in the work, the love that lasts.

And now, my daughter, bright as day,
I see her in a world she'll sway,
With every word and every smile,
I know she carries my mother,
But not just her,
All her cousins, too, reflect in same.
The kindness, love, and strength we share,
The legacy of hearts that care.

Her gentle heart, her giving soul,
Her spirit deep, her love, her goal.
They, too, will carry on this way,
Through them, maa's legacy will stay.

And so, I thank my, mother dear,
For all the gifts she gave, so clear—
For every lesson that she taught,
For all the kindness she had brought.
For showing me how to love and live,
And for the strength to always give.

Now, as I raise my own, I see,
The seeds she planted, grow in me.
The roots and wings she gave to me,
Are the roots and wings I now decree,
To my own daughter, bright and true—
And the other three, too, as I view.

Seeds of Abundance

I was young, eager for space,
In that one-room house, I longed for grace.
Old passbooks, diaries, piled high,
In Papa's briefcase, they'd quietly lie.

One day, I asked, "Let's clear this mess,
Throw out the old things, and make it less."
She smiled and opened that heavy case,
To share with me, her secret place.

With patience, she read each entry through,
And gave me lessons, simple but true:
"Money that comes—be it small or grand,
It shouldn't just stay, but grow as planned."

"From salary, pension, gifts so small,
We have bills, rent, and fees to call.
Groceries, school fees—these we must pay,
But saving, my child, is the only way."

"Two rupees, just two, is all we need,
No matter how tough, or what life may breed.
In a bank or scheme, we'll place them with care,
In two months, they'll grow, and more we'll share."

At that time, the numbers didn't make sense,
Her talk of savings felt so immense.
But her wisdom went beyond the math,
And somehow, I knew she was on the right path.

We had little, yet she saved with grace,
Through years of hardship, she kept up the pace.
And one day, with tired eyes, she sighed,
Saying, "I want one thing before I die:

A house of my own, my own little place,
Where I don't have to move, or keep up the race.
Just a place to call home, with walls so wide,
A roof that's ours, where we can reside."

Her dream wasn't just for bricks and stone,
It was a future where we'd never be alone.
Her dream was simple: to give us our best,
A life of abundance, and peaceful rest.

So, while she saved, and scraped, and planned,
She built a life with steady hand.
Her *one selfish dream* wasn't just for a house,
But for the family she'd always espoused.

Now I walk through rooms, both big and bright,
I think of those days with heart full of light.
From those two rupees, carefully saved,
A home was built, a future paved.

I look at our house, the wide veranda,
And remember her quiet, humble agenda.
She wanted one thing—yes, a home to call hers,
But more than that, a legacy that endures.

Her method was simple, her wisdom was clear,
She knew that small steps would lead us here.
And now, I stand with pride and say,
The house we have today is thanks to her way.

Her Voice, Our Guide: Daily Lessons of Love

My day begins with her wisdom shared,
On WhatsApp, without fail, she's there.
Just after dawn, when the world's still new,
She sends her thoughts, both tried and true.

With a few words, or a quote, or a call,
She reaches out, to guide us all.
Three sons, three daughters, four grandkids too,
She keeps us close, though far in view.

She talks to each one, no matter the hour,
Checking in, offering advice, showing her power.
No distance too far, no schedule too tight,
She keeps us all connected, day and night.

Through her, we learn without knowing when,
As she sends her thoughts, again and again.
From kitchen tricks to home-making tips,
She shares the wisdom of life's many flips.

Financial advice, and lessons on grace,
How to keep pace, how to find your place.
She's our teacher, our guide, in all that we do,
A walking institution, always with a clue.

Morally sound, and socially aware,
She teaches us all how to truly care.
How to be humble, and how to be kind,
How to build strength, and peace of mind.

She doesn't need a title or degree,
But in her, I see an educational legacy.

Welcomed By Your Love

With open arms, you took us in,
Not just as guests, but next of kin.
A mother's warmth, a steady guide,
A friend, a teacher by our side.

From kitchens warm to children's care,
We learned each skill you taught with flair.
What we know now, we owe to you—
In every task, you led us through.

You showed us that we, too, could soar,
Urged us to dream, and seek for more.
"You've studied hard, now go, achieve,
Stand tall, be strong, and just believe."

You've shown resilience, strength so rare,
A quiet power, a love so fair.
We see in you the will to rise,
A spark that lights and never dies.

And as for me, your son-in-law,
I've marveled, watched in quiet awe,
Your wisdom bright in all you do,
In spending wise and saving, too.

A life so balanced, so refined,
A mind both gentle, firm, aligned,
With every golden rule you give,
You teach us all the ways to live.

A woman strong, both fierce and kind,
In you, a wealth of grace we find.
Thank you, Mother, for the way you share,
A heart so full, beyond compare.

Forever grateful, here we stand,
With love and pride, we hold your hand.

-Neha, Manisha and Digvijay

From the Sons' Hearts

There's nothing more that we could need,
Than the love you gave, the life you freed.
From the very start, you showed the way,
Guided us forward every day.

Your strength, your courage, your quiet might,
Built our world, turned wrong to right.
In every challenge, you stood tall,
Teaching us to rise, to never fall.

Whatever we've achieved, all that we know,
It's you who helped our spirits grow.
From every lesson, every task,
It's you who taught us, no need to ask.

You're the reason we stand so strong,
The reason we've made it all along.
In you, we found a steady light,
A mother's love, forever bright.

You've shaped us both, with endless care,
In every choice, you're always there.
Your wisdom, your far-sighted grace,
Has built our lives, has set our pace.

Your courage to learn, to rise above,
Taught us the meaning of strength and love.
You showed us how to face our fears,
How to chase dreams, and wipe our tears.

We've been called your Ram and Lakshman true,
And with that name, we've learned from you.
It's more than a bond, it's responsibility,
To carry your legacy, your humility.

But how do we fill shoes so wide?
How do we carry what you've supplied?
You've done the impossible, made it all real,
A journey of strength, a force we feel.

We look at this life, and often say,
How could we walk without your way?
For without you, the path would be lost,
You're the reason we count each cost.

You're the heart, the soul, the core,
Without you, we are nothing more.
We adore you, love you, and hold you dear,
Our mother, our strength, forever near.

In all we do, you're in our hearts,
Your legacy lives in every part.
The impossible you've made so true,
And we give all the credit to you.

- Manish and Sidharth

A Circle of Love: The Many Voices of Admiration

In every corner, her love has spread,
A ripple that grows, and keeps ahead.
The wisdom she shares, the strength she shows,
Is seen and felt wherever she goes.

Her heart, her kindness, a shining light,
A beacon of grace, so pure and bright.
And as I pause, and take a breath,
I think of those who hold her close, and feel blessed.

They speak of her with words so kind,
And always with respect, so intertwined.
They call her strong, they call her wise,
A soul so gentle, it lights the skies.

Suman, from the office, calls her Maa,
And says, "She's a mother to me, a guide, a mentor, always
steady, always free."
Virender Chachu and *Manju Chachi* show immense respect
and pride,
And once told me, "Bhabhi ji, you are an institution, with
wisdom far and wide."

Suman Maami proudly shares the bond of love,
Stronger than blood, she says, "Your mother is the only one
after God that I confide in, my dove."
Tau ji and many other relatives often say,
"Just be your mama's shadow, and you'll shine in every
way."

My *mother-in-law* speaks with praise, so happy and bright,
"Your mother never sits idle, always thinking, always doing,
always right.
May God keep making souls like hers, full of grace,
An inspiration for all, lighting every place."

In sonepat, Satish mausa ji, ashwini, kailash mausa ji and
others say, "she is our *iron lady* with strength so rare, both
fierce and steady, a humble heart , yet bold and true". They
all being so humble and successful themselves say, we
admire her in all she'd do"

And her colleagues, kamlesh aunty, jyoti aunty, veena
aunty, *Meena aunty, Shashi aunty*, and *Santosh aunty*,
All hold her in the highest esteem, their admiration never
runs empty.
*Inderjeet aunty, Sunil aunty, Tarak Bhaiya, and Virender
uncle,* too,
Show love and respect, though their paths have split, their
hearts remain true.

Even after time and distance have grown,
They feel her presence, and call her their own.
No matter where life leads, they'll never part,
For her love and wisdom have a permanent place in their
heart.

Her family, too, knows her value and worth,
They've seen her rise, they've seen her birth
The strength to endure, the will to be kind,
A force so powerful, it leaves none behind.

Names and faces I can't all recall,
But every single one has been touched by her call.
So here, I say, as I end this rhyme:
Her influence is felt, through space and time.

Becoming Her

I remember her as a strict mother,
Firm in her ways, yet soft in her heart.
Her love was never loud, never wild,
It was steady, it was quiet, it was pure, like the start.

She taught me the value of grace and poise,
To carry myself with dignity, to speak with a soft voice.
"Be a lady," she'd say, "with kindness and care,"
And in her words, I found a life that was fair.

She was emotional, yes, but that was her strength,
Her heart beat for me at every length.
She held me close when life was tough,
And showed me how love is always enough.

I carry her in my eyes, in the lashes so long,
The same eyes that saw me, the same that were strong.
Her beauty passed down, in every glance,
A legacy of light, a beautiful chance.

When grey strands first appeared in my hair,
She took it on herself, with love and care.
Amla, shikakai, and bhringraaj she'd soak,
For me, she'd treat my hair like gold—no joke.

She'd tell me, "Never waste, save what you can,"
Her wisdom, like seeds, planted a plan.
"Especially food," she'd say, "it's not just to eat,
It's a blessing to cherish, every meal is sweet."

Her lessons ran deeper than words alone,
She taught me to share, to make kindness known.
To listen, to understand, to never talk back,
When others are angry, don't add to the attack.

"Think of others first," she always says,
In doing so, you'll never be misled.
Her words were simple, yet shaped who I am,
Her guidance is the thread in the life I've planned.

But her love isn't just in words, it was in the stand she took,
In every choice I made, in every path I took.
When I joined NCC, or performed on stage,
When I followed paths that none has dared engage,

She stood by me, though others would doubt,
When all were against me, she'd speak out.
She was scared of the consequences, of what could go wrong,
But she trusted the morals she'd taught me all along.

Her love wasn't loud, but it was fierce and true,
It was the strength to let me be, to let me break through.
She'd fear the unknown, but still, she'd stand tall,
Believing in me, believing in the values that never fall.

So many times, she made tough calls alone,
Scared, unsure, but always shown
That her belief in me, in the life she had sown,
Was the anchor, the truth, the love she had known.

Her love was in those moments, quiet yet clear,
In every decision made with a heart full of fear.
She wasn't just guiding me, she was guiding my way,
With a belief that would never sway.

Now, I see it in myself, that quiet, steady force,
That belief in values, in taking my course.
She took the hard steps, trusting in what's right,
Her way of loving, silent but bright.

And I know that this love she gave, this strength she instilled,
Is the reason I stand strong, my dreams fulfilled.

Now, I see her in me, in all that I do,
Her strength, her grace, her love, so true.
I'm blessed with qualities she passed down to me,
A happier, better human, because I can see.

And I watch her qualities in my own children's eyes,
In how they share, in how they empathize.
Unintentionally, she's passed on the light,
Her legacy shining, like stars in the night.

I may have grown, but I'll always remain,
Her daughter, with her in my heart, like a gentle refrain.
For everything I am, everything I've become,
I owe it to her — my mother, my moon, my home.

As I walk forward, I carry her light,
In the way I mother, in the way I fight.
To be the same gentle strength, the same love so pure,
To my own children, this legacy shall endure.

I will love them like she loved me,
Guiding them softly, helping them see,
That grace and kindness will always be true,
And the world is better when we care for you.

I'll be a good daughter, as she is to hers,
In every way that her love assures.
Her lessons, her values, I'll continue to teach,
With every gesture, with every reach.

For, I am her reflection, and in her shadow, I stand,
A mother, a child, with love in my hands.
Her legacy is my legacy too,
To be a good human, in all I do.